iPhones 8 and X

New Features and How-to-Use Guide

Table of Contents

INTRODUCTION

CHAPTER ONE: RELEASE OF IPHONE X AND IPHONE 8

CHAPTER TWO: UNIQUE FEATURES OF IPHONE X AND IPHONE 8

CHAPTER THREE: THE DIFFERENCE BETWEEN IPHONE X AND IPHONE 8

CHAPTER FOUR: GETTING STARTED WITH THE NEW FEATURES OF THE LATEST IPHONES IN TOWN

CHAPTER FIVE: THE BENEFITS OF INVESTING IN THE LATEST IPHONES 8 AND X

CHAPTER SIX: THE COMMON TROUBLESHOOTING SOLUTIONS FOR THE IPHONES 8 AND X

CONCLUSION

Other Technology Books by the Author Ben Alexi

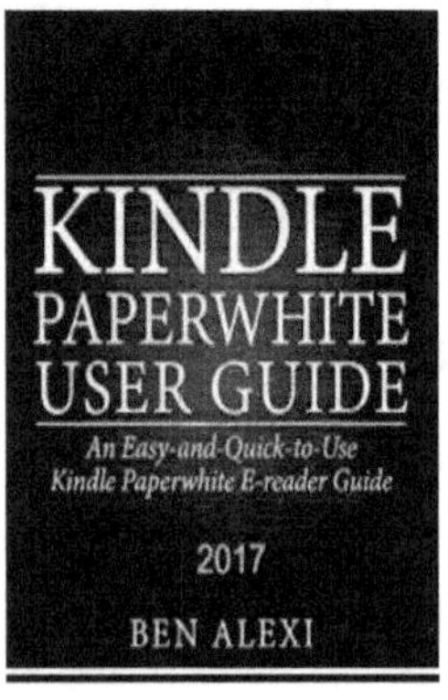

INTRODUCTION

Following the historical conversation between the Motorola engineer Marty Cooper and Joel Engel using a portable cell phone, mobile phones are dramatically evolving. From the rise of SMS to anywhere, mobile photography to anytime internet, the magical mobile technology cases are an essential part of communication between members of the global society. Ever since the invention, 41 years ago, the handsets have acted as a catalyst for both the technological and the cultural changes. With no sign of slowing down the innovation, iPhone was born on June 29, 2007. From then, the iPhone owners usually have an easy upgrade decision every year.

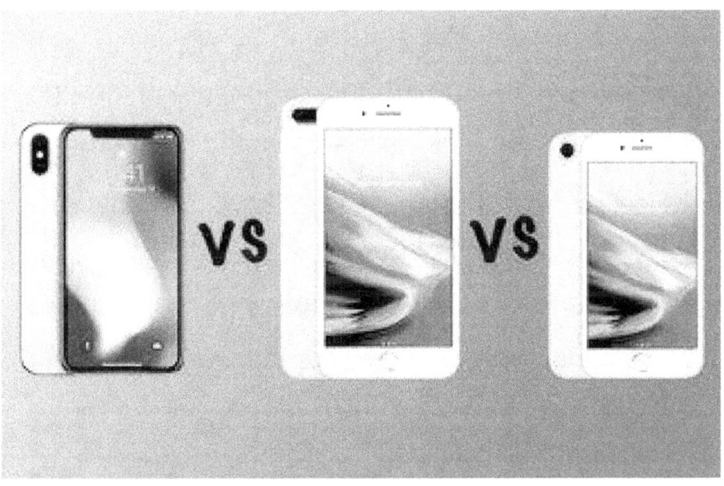

The upgrades come with either regular screens or the iPhone plus with a bigger display. On September this year, therefore, the company has announced three brand new models with specific properties in order to meet the different tastes of the current market: the iPhone X, iPhone 8 and the iPhone 8 plus. According to the reports from the professional mobile phone handlers, the iPhone X is Apple's best iPhone release.

The Apple iPhone X vs. iPhone 8 Plus vs iPhone 8

The features, therefore, of the latest releases match the price tags on them. Understanding the features of the phones make it easier for the users to select the one that matches their individual tastes. For this reason, this book includes a chapter that describes, in detail, the features of both the iPhone X and the iPhone 8 handsets for an easy selection as either a birthday or wedding present. Regardless of the similar features to the iPhone 7 and the iPhone 7 Plus, going through the outstanding properties of the handsets would drive you into buying them for a memorable experience.

The release of the latest Apple phones follows the ever-competitive global market for more aesthetic and technological handsets. This consideration ensures that the users bring the world close to them and as well enhance their business for a blooming economic growth throughout the entire globe. Other than facilitating business, the revolutionary design of the newest Apple products makes it convenient for their lovers to utilize the content of the without any inconvenience.

All the three releases have specific properties that make each of them different from the others. This provides the reason why either of the releases is recommendable for the different lovers of Apple products depending on the needs they need to meet through using the gadget. The different features as well provide the varying prices regardless of the fact that all the three are of the same generation.

Special instructions on how to utilize the gadgets and its features for a productive society with reliable communication networks. The instruction also includes the management principles that ensures maximum utilization of the properties. Proper management of the gadgets ensures that the products last long enough to ensure the Apple lovers get the best from the preferred gadgets.

In addition to the management principles, having the information about the tricks and shortcuts to ensure easy navigation through the gadget helps the faster realization of the results following the using the Apple products. That is, saving time. It is, therefore, important for any technology-oriented individuals to ensure that they purchase this book and make use of its content for a memorable mobile phone experience.

Get a copy, therefore, of this book and go through its content as the first step in enjoying the outstanding features of the latest Apple products, and as a result get close to the future touchscreen handsets that are lighter, wider, resistant to their environment and more powerful. The information in this book is, therefore, the first step in joining the elite members of the global society.

CHAPTER ONE: RELEASE OF IPHONE X AND IPHONE 8

To mark the 10-year anniversary since launching of the first ever iPhone, the Apple Company introduced three new iPhone models on 12th of September, including the iPhone 8, iPhone 8 Plus and the iPhone X. the latest releases have faster processors as well as better cameras compared to the previous year's iPhone 7 and iPhone 7 Plus. Other than the better cameras and faster processors, the brand new iPhones come with the ability to charge them wirelessly.

As a marketing strategy, the iPhone 8 and iPhone 8 Plus were not released at the same time: the iPhones 8 and 8 Plus were released on 12th September this year but the iPhone X pre-orders began on the 27th October with the official release being on 3rd of November. The iPhone X comes with better features than the earlier iPhones 8 and 8 Plus. For this reason, the prices do not match.

After the official shipping of all the three-iPhone models, Apple makes the gadgets available to its customers through its iPhone Upgrade Program, with the monthly payment of a minimum of 56.45 pounds. In the United States, however, the pricing of the 64GB and 256GB configuration iPhone X starts at around $999 and the $1,149 respectively.

The Carphone warehouse provides the latest iPhones at retailer prices to the global users. Pre-ordering of the gadgets is required, therefore, to acquire the gadget.

The EE site also provides the online store from where the users can pre-order the handset. All the plans in this site comes with up to six free months of Apple Music as well as free data. To make it convenient for the customers, the online platform has launched a registration page for the interested customers.

Apple has instructed the suppliers of the components to withhold shipment of some of the components used to produce the iPhone X devices during this first year. Reports suggest that the chain-supply partners shipped components amounting to only 40% of the planned quantity for the production of the gadgets.

This ordering of the under-shipment of components is similar to what happened during the production of the iPhone 7 during the previous year when Apple instructed the producers to produce only the initial 60% of the total components for the production of the gadget.

Due to the production of the fewer components for the production of the iPhone X, the stock is expected to meet the customers demand during the 2018 year following the release of all the components planned by the Apple Company. Similarly, the iPhones 8 and 8 Plus, being released earlier, are more available compared to the bigger iPhone X.

The pricing of the latest iPhones into the market is inclusive of a VAT of up to 20 percent as well as an Insurance Premium Tax (where applicable). The shipping cost, however, is not taken into consideration during the pricing strategies.

During the first three months of the year 2018, the Apple Company rectified the shipment issue of its latest products to ensure that the supply meet the global demand. In connection to this, the different companies dealing with the handsets have announced their interest to display the new iPhone models for access to their esteemed clients. For example, the UK operator Three has made it clear that it would offer all the three new Apple products.

Vodafone is another company that has shown interest in dealing with the three latest iPhones. Both the O2 and the Virgin Mobile Companies have confirmed that they will begin selling all the iPhones 8, 8 Plus and the X handsets to their clients.

Following the reports that the Apple Company has produced the latest iPhones 8, 8 Plus and the X, the market describes 2017 as the supercycle of iPhone (a large number of existing iPhone users upgrading).

The Apple Company through Ming-Chi Kuo has; however, argue that the real supercycle was in the year 2018 because of the following reasons:

a) Addressing the TrueDepth Camera production issue will be done in 2018F

b) Longer sales period expected in 2018F compared to 2017

c) The designs in 2018F will be competitive compared to 2017 when the first stock was let into the market. That is, the iPhone shipment in 2017 is expected to come in at between 210-220mn units and should grow to about 245-255mn units in 2018.

Other than the already launched iPhones 8 and 8 Plus, rumors have it that the Apple Company would introduce at least two OLED iPhones in the coming 2018 year. The gadgets would measure at 5.85in and 6.46in respectively.

The two expected OLED iPhones X in 2018

As Apple Company enjoy the mouthwatering profits out of its flagship iPhone X, Samsung Company will also be making cash for supplying the OLED displays, capacitors, and batteries to be used for the iPhone X gadget.

Reports by the Counterpoint Technology Market Research carried out for the Wall Street Journal indicated that Samsung is likely to gain up to $4bn revenue without adding the amount out of the sales of the flagship Galaxy devices.

Considering the environmental issues that negatively affect the quality of global lives, Apple Company has introduced the green credentials of its latest products.

That is, the material used to design the smartphones are free from the mercury, PVC as well as arsenic.

The fact that the fibers are sourced from either the managed bamboo, forest, recycled paper or the waste sugarcane make it favorable for the environment. The amount of greenhouse gas emission during the entire lifecycle of the iPhones 8, 8 Plus and X.

Although it is normal that the stock of new iPhones are always limited after the official launching, this time around the stock is extremely below the usual deficiency following the launching of the previous iPhones. Despite the unusual deficiencies, Apple Company expects that by January 2018 enough devices would be made available to all the admirers of the three brand new iPhone gadgets.

CHAPTER TWO: UNIQUE FEATURES OF IPHONE X AND IPHONE 8

With the metallic band around the devices edges and beautiful all-glass bodies, the latest Apple releases are visually attractive to the customers. The aesthetic nature of the iPhones come with outstanding features that rectify the mistakes in order to match the recommended demand of the iPhone lovers. With the excellent properties signifying the latest iPhones 8, 8 Plus and the X, including the luxurious-feeling of the gadgets makes them more powerful compared to the previous models.

Of all the iPhones ever let into the market, the latest Apple products are the cheapest considering the feature that is included. As an illustration, the iPhone 8 comes with a lower price compared to the iPhone X due to additional features that are included. Understanding the features of the three latest releases is vital in the selection of the most favorable one for the user based on either the financial capability or the purpose for which you desire to use the phone. This chapter, therefore, discusses all the knockout properties that trigger the iPhone users with the desire to upgrade.

1. **The design and the display**

The vision of the Apple Company has always been to come up with an iPhone gadget that is made of glass all over. That is the iPhone X. the iPhones 8 and the 8 Plus, on the other hand, are similar to the traditional iPhone models. Taking into consideration the different individual tastes of the Apple products lovers, the latest iPhones come in varying colors: space grey, silver, the orange tone, pinkish shade as well as the gold shading.

The three latest iPhone releases come in different super retina display sizes. That is, the iPhone 8 features a 4.7-inch display, the 8 Plus has 5.5-inch display while the iPhone X comes with up to 5.8-inch display. Just the same as the one introduced in the iPad Pro, the new iPhones include the True Tone that makes use of the ambient light sensor in order to detect lighting inside a room as well as adjusting the color temperature and the intensity in order to match the light for a more natural and memorable viewing experience.

Apple uses a seven-layer ink process in order to add color to the glass to give the iPhone gadgets a rich depth of color. An oleophobic coating makes it easier for wiping away of either the smudges or the fingerprints. An ion-strengthened glass used to design the display, additionally, is tough enough to break in case the special maintenance procedures are taken into keen considerations.

The Apple devices are characterized by a glass shell and display held together by a stainless steel internal frame and an aerospace-grade 7000 Series aluminum band that matches the color of the iPhone. This match gives the device a seamless appearance. For adequate signal, small and nearly invisible antenna lines that cut through the aluminum frame. The iPhones offer support for the P3 wide color for a rich, 625 cd/m2 max brightness and a true-to-life colors. This feature is identical to the earlier iPhones 7 and 7 Plus.

2. Battery life and the inductive wireless charging

The long-term users of the iPhones complain about the initial iPhone battery lives. The company, in response to these complains, has improved the battery lives of the thee latest devices that aim at transforming the communication and business world. To ascertain this point, a Chinese regulatory filing has revealed that the iPhone X, for example, has a capacity of up to 2,716mAh. The measurements compare to the 1,821mAh in the iPhone 8 and the 2,675mAh in the iPhone 8 Plus.

Following the fulltime use of the iPhones in addition to the iOS 11has made it difficult to solve the battery life issue. With the aim of making them more reliable and attractive, the iPhones 8, 8 Plus and the X have the ability to charge wirelessly. This new invention has reduced the number of hours that the iPhones have been left on the socket walls to recharge. The phone takes only about a half an hour when it is put to the

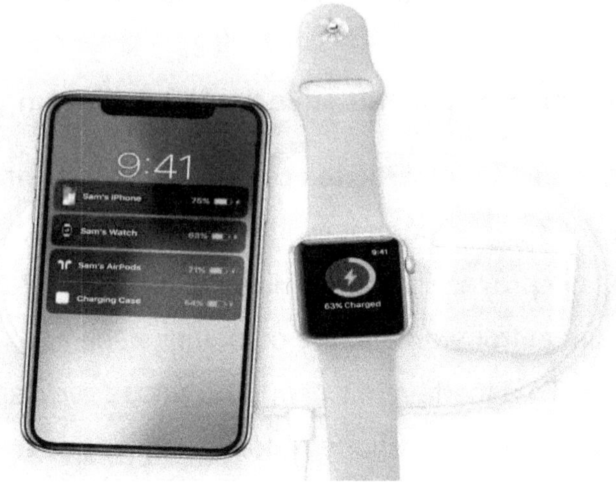

USB-C fast charger. The period depends on how busy the user is busy with his or her gadget.

An iPhone X, AirPods (in An AirPods case) and Apple watch on a wireless AirPower

The glass body of the gadgets allows for the inductive wireless charging feature. Because of the adoption of the Qi-certified charging standard, the latest iPhones in the market. Recharging is enabled following a physical contact between the device on either a charging mat or a similar accessory. The gadget is simply placed on the accessory.

With the Qi charging standards have been available for several years now, there are many wireless charging accessories available on the market. Companies like the Mophie and Belkin, for example, deal with the chargers specifically for the Apple devices.

To make it even more convenient, Apple is planning to develop, by 2018, multiple devices charging technology called **AirPower**.

Examples of wireless charging accessories.

3. The outstanding A11 Bionic Processor

Better than in any previous smartphone, the three latest iPhones come with an A11 Bionic processor that features a six-core CPU: two high-performance cores as well as four high-efficiency cores. This property makes the iPhones more powerful and efficient. The two A11 cores are 25% faster compared to the A10 chip found in the earlier iPhone 7 with the four high-efficiency cores rating up to 70% faster. Reports indicate that the neural engine is capable of supporting up to 600 billion operations every second.

Using a second-generation performance controller, all the four cores can be harnessed simultaneously. This contributes to up to 70% better performance for a multi-threaded workflow within an Apple device. Favorably, the A11 chip includes a new Apple-designed three-core CPU believed to be 30% faster compared to the GPU included in the A10 chip. This Apple-design improves the graphics performance.

The chip also includes also an embedded M11 Motion coprocessor that allows for the capturing of the motion-based data from either the gyroscope, compass or accelerometer. This ability powers the fitness capabilities and augmented reality experiences in apps and games without having to drain significant power.

To improve the speed and performance of the gadgets, the latest iPhones come with a RAM of up to 2GB for the iPhone 8 and the 3GB for both the iPhone 8 Plus and the iPhone X. The additional features, including the dual-lens camera, confirms the need for more RAM in either the iPhones 8 Plus and X.

An additional adaptive recognition supported by the A11 chip allows for Face ID feature in the iPhone X model. This adaptation to physical changes in the user's appearance happens over time.

4. Upgrading to the iOS 11

With A10 chip being the most powerful operating system for the mobile devices, the A11 sets a new standard to make the iPhones better than before. The operating system allows the device to function as a computer since it gives it the much-needed Control Center reorganization.

With the operating system made available to all the iPhone users, the following procedure is vital for those who would desire to upgrade:

- ❖ The first procedure entails backing up your gadget to ensure you do not lose the important data.
- ❖ The next step involves updating the gadget wirelessly. In case of the difficulties updating the device wirelessly, it is possible to use the iTunes to enjoy the latest iOS update.
- ❖ Upon the installation of the iOS 11, a message appears on your Apple Watch. This prompts the user to upgrade to the watchOS 4.

Before opting to upgrade your iPhone, it is important to ensure that the device is compatible with the iOS 11.

The excellent iOS 11 operating system allows for easy and better multitasking to ensure that the user enjoys a memorable experience when it comes to using the Apple products. Upgrading to the iOS 11 comes with benefits such as the Siri getting a more natural-sounding voice (the user has the ability to select between the male and female voice options). It is also easier to see the older alerts that the user has missed since the lock screen notification and the notification center have become one in the iOS 11. An additional Do Not Disturb While Driving feature in the iOS 11 limits the number of road accidents because the user has the privilege of driving without distraction.

Unfortunately, the new iOS 11 comes with some issues that limit the navigation through the contents of the iPhones:

- ✓ Battery drain is still an issue upon upgrading to a better operating system.
- ✓ Both the Bluetooth and Wi-Fi issues due to the inability of the Control Center to disable the Wi-Fi and Bluetooth from the quick settings toggles.
- ✓ The operating system is compatible only with phones that have the ability to run the 64-bit chipset (first introduced with the iPhone 5S).

5. Outstanding camera: simplified art of photography

To enhance the photography art, the latest iPhone releases come with larger and faster camera sensors. New color filters and deeper pixels are some of the properties that have improved the camera experience for the lovers of the Apple device. The ability of the camera to shoot videos in 4K has made it a good purchase for the Apple company customers. The phones include both the front and rear cameras. Both the iPhone 8 Plus and the iPhone X have dual cameras on the rear side. This positioning of the lenses allows for snapping of quality images using the portrait mode that artfully blurs the background of the image. For the iPhone X, for example, each of the dual-lenses has about 12Mp and with the ability to offer optical image stabilization. One of the cameras has an aperture of f/1.8 while the other one is having f/2.4.

The camera of the iPhones uses the "stage light" process to allow editing of the images. This is enabled by the ability of the feature to cast realistic light on the object to be pictured. The lenses are paired with new LED True Tone Flash with Slow Sync designed to offer a more natural lighting.

A 7Mp TrueDepth camera is located on the front of the phone to allow for selfies and the Face ID (limited to iPhone X). For advanced face mapping, the TrueDepth camera is made of a flood illuminator, infrared camera as well as a dot projector.

Limited to the iPhones 8 Plus and 7, the rear cameras allows application of the portrait mode. IPhone X, however, allows the users' to use the portrait mode on both the rear and front cameras. An outstanding Portrait Lighting feature offers five different lighting styles that help in the improvement of portraits further.

To allow for motion tracking, the A11 Bionic chip designs the iPhone X's camera for AR, with the new accelerometers and gyroscopes.

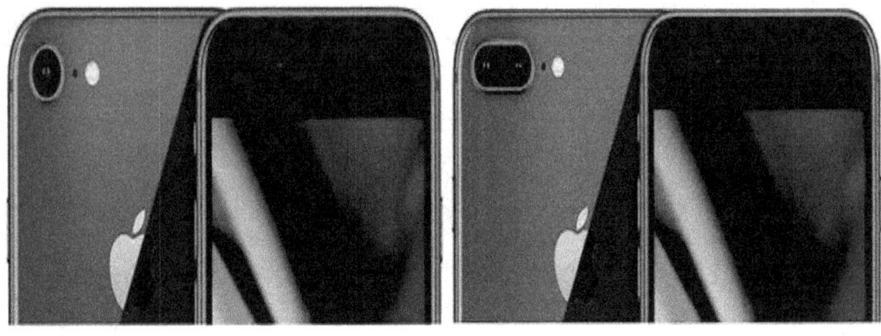

In addition to the front cameras, the iPhone 8 has a single 12MP rear camera while the iPhone 8 Plus has dual-lens rear cameras.

Just like the other two iPhones (8 and 8 Plus), the iPhone X also includes a front camera that is vital for facial recognition as well as for quality selfies.

6. Resistant to water

Similar to the iPhones of the previous generation, the Apple Company has ensured that all the three latest devices introduced into the market are both water and dust resistant. A rating of IP67 dust/water resistance shows that the two devices are entirely dustproof and can withstand one meter of water immersion (3.3 feet) for up to 30 minutes.

Even with this property attractive, intentional exposure of the gadget to water should be avoided at all cost. The manufacturers of the product (Apple Company) warns that the property is temporary because of the normal wear of the iPhone. To make it even worse, the company's warranty does not cover any kind of water damage to the iOS device. *iPhones 8 Plus and 8 withstand light soaking*

Additional features that make the latest iPhone the best buys in town

Other than the features that have been highlighted above, other properties are included by the Apple Company to ensure it remains competitive in the limited market:

❖ **Speakers**

The latest gadgets come with two redesigned stereo speakers that are up to 25 percent louder than those found in the previous iPhones 7 and 7 Plus. The speakers have the additional deeper bass that ensures the user enjoys the rhythm of any song. One of the speakers is found at the top while the other one at the bottom.

❖ **LTE**

This feature is a relief for those iPhone users that like traveling. That is, the up to 20 LTE bands that are available in the latest iPhones advances the data transfer speeds up to 450Mb/s. This property allows the devices to work well with networks in other countries during the locomotion. This is unlike the earlier iPhones 7 and 7 Plus that used both the Intel and Qualcomm chips (some not compatible with the CDMA network of the Sprint and Verizon in the United States.

❖ **Wi-Fi**

Similar to the Wi-Fi technology in the iPhones 7 and 7 Plus that had a connection speed of up to a theoretical maximum of 866Mb/s, the latest iPhones in town supports 802.11a/b/g/n/ac Wi-Fi with MIMO

❖ **The Bluetooth, NFC and GPS**

The latest iPhones 8, 8 Plus and X support a new 5.0 Bluetooth that offers up to four times the range, eight times the broadcast message capacity and two times the speed compared to the earlier Bluetooth 4.2 standard in the older releases.

Other than the ability to support the Global Positioning System (GPS) operated by the United States government, the three latest iPhones support the Europe's QZSS and Global Satellite Navigation System, Galileo as well as the Quasi-Zenith Satellite System that is used in Japan. The Galileo support allows a precise positioning following a combination of the GLONASS, GPS, and the Galileo signals. The positioning, therefore, has a modern signal structure that makes the users maintain their position fix while navigating through the globe. Additionally, a new NFC chip has a reader mode support letting the devices read NFC tags that are installed in places such as the museums, retail stores and more.

CHAPTER THREE: THE DIFFERENCE BETWEEN IPHONE X AND IPHONE 8

Apple's decision to ditch iPhone 7 Plus for the iPhones 8 and the 8 Plus came because of subsequent complains about the products. To the global surprise, the company decided to introduce another brand designed specifically to mark its 10th-anniversary celebration. With features similar to that of the iPhones 8 and 8 plus, this iPhone X comes with some features that are make them a special and outstanding purchase. The difference in features also provides the users with a variety of options to choose from when they decide to acquire an iPhone for either their personal or rather commercial use. Having gone through the excellent features of the latest three smartphones in the second chapter, this part of the book highlights the features that make the iPhone X different from both the iPhones 8 and 8 Plus:

A. The iPhone X retail box

Starting from packaging, the latest iPhone X is packaged with the screen facing up. This screen-up display of the device shows that much focus is put on the improvement done on the device's (albeit notched) display.

This packaging is unlike that of the remaining iPhones already in the market, with their screens facing down.

Inside the retail box, however, the following contents are found:

- The iPhone X with iOS 11
- EarPods with Lightning Connector
- Lightning to 3.5 mm Headphone Jack Adapter
- Lightning to USB Cable
- USB Power Adapter
- Documentation

B. **The edge-to-edge display with a stunning 5.8-inch Super Retina display with an OLED panel**

The iPhone X has a bigger display (about 5.8-inch) that comes in a small overall form design. That is, the smartphone is a bit bigger than the iPhone 8 considering the dimensions. However, it has lesser dimension than the 8 Plus (10mm bigger) making it fairly comfortable to hold using one hand. The display is different from the bezels that are found in the other iPhone available on the market.

Edge-to-edge screen of the iPhone X

The screen of this outstanding smartphone comes with a million-to-one contrast ratio and a wide color support. The availability of HDR, as a component, allows the device to support both the HDR10 and the Dolby Vision. This enables the Apple Company to keep the healthy competition with its rivals like the LG and Samsung companies.

At the top of its screen, the iPhone X features a notch that creates room for the speaker, front camera, the infrared camera for facial recognition and a flood illuminator among several other features.

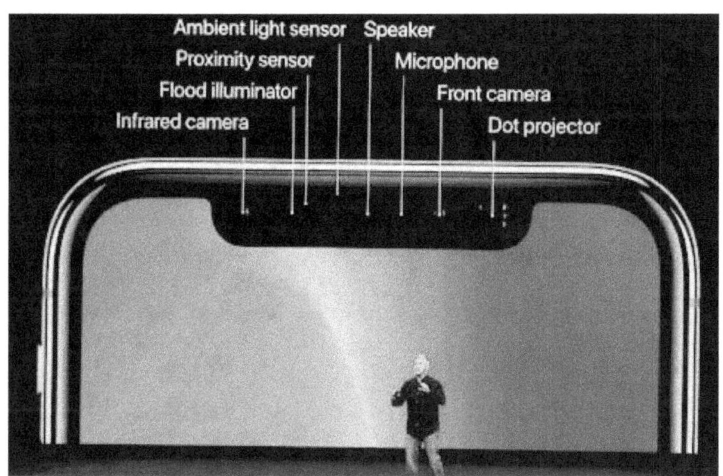

Features at the notch at the top of iPhone X screen

Other than just being large, Apple Company considered the OLED technology to give the iPhone X an excellent display. This display gives the iPhone a much greater contrast ratio compared to that on the iPhone 8 (with the usual LCD IPS display). The OLED display offers the user with perfect blacks and more attractive colors than the LCD displays. The vivid colors come because of the higher resolution of 2,436 x 1,125 pixels.

C. The facial recognition ability

A major difference between the iPhones X and 8 is the lack of TouchID and the home button. Instead, the X smartphone houses a FaceID feature that scans the users' faces when unlocking the phone. The property is also important when using the Apple Pay.

The iPhones FaceID system

To enhance the privacy of the user, the secure enclave protects all the facial data. However, all the processing is done in the on-device and not in the cloud.

In addition to the outstanding FaceID, a clever TrueDepth camera located on the front of the iPhone X to make the users enjoy the exceptional Animojis feature that brings some popular emojis to real life. That is, the camera works with the A11 Bionic to analyze up to 50 different movements of the facial muscle in order to animate the expressions in different Animojis, including a robot, panda, and unicorn.

An Apple iPhone X Animoji mimicking an expression

The animated characters are saved in the iMessage app to enable the users to record and send Animoji messages to their various contacts. This special property, fortunately, will be coming to third party apps like the Snapchat that allows the user to send more detailed emoji.

D. Advantages for the purchase of an iPhone 8 over the iPhone X

In terms of what they offer, the iPhones X and 8 are quite different. For example, the design, features, the pricing and the important e display size among other. However, they offer similar internal specs. This means that they both offer similar performance experiences.

Importantly, long-term and experienced iPhone users explain the various facts as to why the iPhone 8 is more advantageous than the iPhone X:

❖ Despite the difference in price, the functionalities of both the phones are identical. This functional similarity is so because both the models are powered by the

Apple's neural engine, the M11 motion coprocessor and the A11 Bionic. It is, therefore, advisable to pay less for the iPhone 8 but fulfill their desire.

* Being less known, the FaceID that replaces the TouchID is not proven effective in storing passwords, using the Apple Pay and unlocking the phones. For example, it is not certain that the FaceID feature will work or rather recognize any change in the users' faces.

* All the three iPhones: 8, 8 Plus and the X supports the Qi wireless charging as well as the fast-charging properties. In need of enjoying this property, economists argue that it is prudent to consider the purchase of the iPhone 8 over the 10th anniversary-designed iPhone X.

* The iPhone X is more expensive compared to the iPhone 8 model. The cost of the X smartphone starts at $1,000, while the iPhone 8 goes for only $800. Go, therefore, for the iPhone 8 (still a brand-new release) and save up to $200.

* For the selfie lovers, it is wise to purchase the iPhone 8, which has a front-facing camera that has similar properties to that of the iPhone X (both produce 7-megapixel snaps that have a f/2.2 aperture and a video film in 1080p). Unfortunately, with the iPhone 8 the users will not be able to enjoy some exclusive software

camera features such as the portrait Mode that the front-camera of the iPhone X utilizes.

* ❖ The iPhone 8 does not include the "ugly" notch at the top of the phone screen.

All the three latest releases are modern phones that put attention to the advancement of technology. It is, therefore, important to go through the differences between the iPhones and select the one that satisfies your desire and as well matches your economic status.

CHAPTER FOUR: GETTING STARTED WITH THE NEW FEATURES OF THE LATEST PHONES IN TOWN

You have apparently come to a decision to acquire one of the three latest Apple smartphones (the iPhones 8, 8 Plus and X) having been impressed with the wonderful upgrade features that accompany them. Before you begin enjoying your buy, however, it is advisable to understand some essential things that have to be done right before enjoying the outstanding properties of the devices.

This section of the book highlights the tips, in addition to the basic guideline by the Apple Company, to enable you to enjoy the memorable experience of the devices within a short duration upon its acquisition by the Apple product lovers. The information herein is applicable, no matter which model you prefer.

Restoring from a backup of the previous iPhone is the first step in enjoying the outstanding Apple releases. This process is important if you may desire to keep the important data from your old device. Therefore, the backup should be up-to-date. The backing up process of the content can be done either by the help of the iCloud o the iTunes.

i.   **ICloud backup**

For an iCloud backup, there is no need to connect the iPhone to your Mac. To proceed with the backing up process, simply tap on the **Settings** then select the **Apple ID profile listing** (located at the top). From this point, click the **iCloud** then **iCloud Backup** and finally the **Back up now**. When setting up any of the three latest iPhones, restore the iPhone from this backup upon logging into your brand-new gadget with your individual Apple ID.

Automatic setup is applicable when your old iPhone already supports the iOS 11.the automated setting procedure allows the users to copy across your Apple ID and the home Wi-Fi setting from the other phone by simply placing them close to each other and follow the prompts.

ii.   The iTunes backup

To begin the backing up process, connect the old iPhone to your Mac and launch the iTunes. Choose your iPhone by clicking a little phone icon in the toolbar. Under the **Backups**, select This Computer. The next step involves checking the **Encrypt local backup** in order to ensure that the account passwords and the Health data are backed up as well. Tap the **Back up now** icon to confirm the process. Once the backup process is done, restoring from the backup follows by connecting your new iPhone gadget.

Backing up your old iPhone using an encrypted backup in

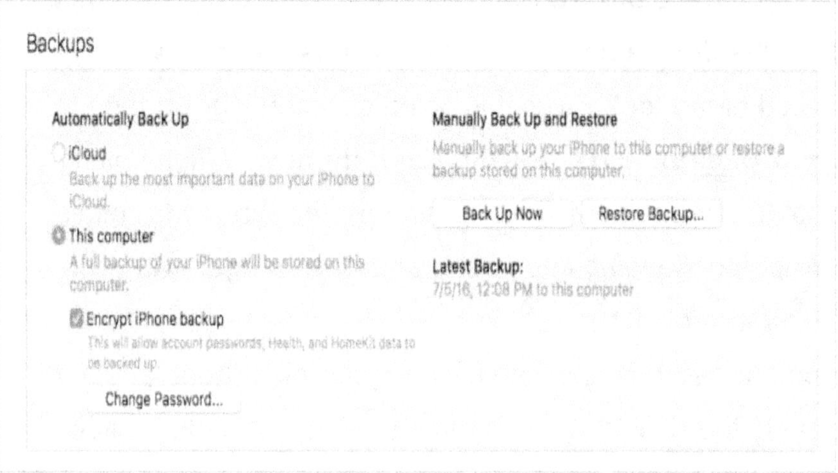

iTunes

For the first time users of iPhones, the Android phone includes a Move from iOS Android app that helps in setting up of the users' Google account data in Mail, Contacts, transferring the Chrome bookmarks to safari, Calendars as well as moving their camera roll over.

The information that follows is vital for the esteemed customers of the Apple products in order to set up their iPhones from scratch. For those who restore their backup, it is vital to ensure they get the best out of their handset.

I.   Turning on the battery percentage notification

Nothing is more pleasing than having a display of how much battery is left after usage. Switching the notification on is, therefore, the first step when getting started with your new iPhone handset. To do this, navigate to **<u>Settings</u>** and then click on **<u>Battery</u>**. From this point, a toggle for **<u>Low Power Mode</u>** and that of the **<u>Battery percentage</u>**. Click, therefore, the second option (Battery Percentage) **<u>ON</u>** to give you the

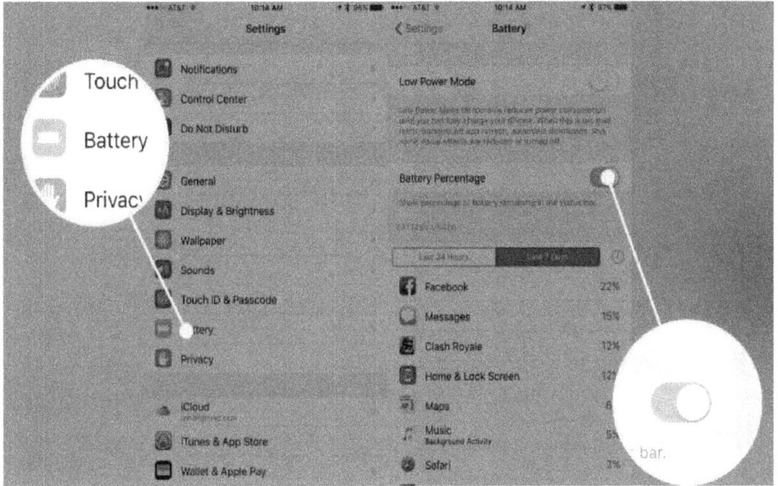

highlight of how much energy is left.

Battery percentage has to be switched on

II.   Re-download useful apps

Some apps in your old iPhone might not be important anymore. Such applications need not to be installed on the new phone. A clean set up is, therefore, important to ensure that only the useful apps are re-downloaded. To do this, sign into your Apple account from the App Store app. From the App, download the apps that you have used in the last six months.

III.   Set up the Do Not Disturb

While using your iPhone, distractions such as iMessages and constant notifications usually irritate. To prevent such disturbances, scheduling a Do Not Disturb setting at the times when you do not need to be agitated. To do this, visit the **Settings** app then toggle the Scheduled to **ON** and decide on the duration of time that you do not wish for

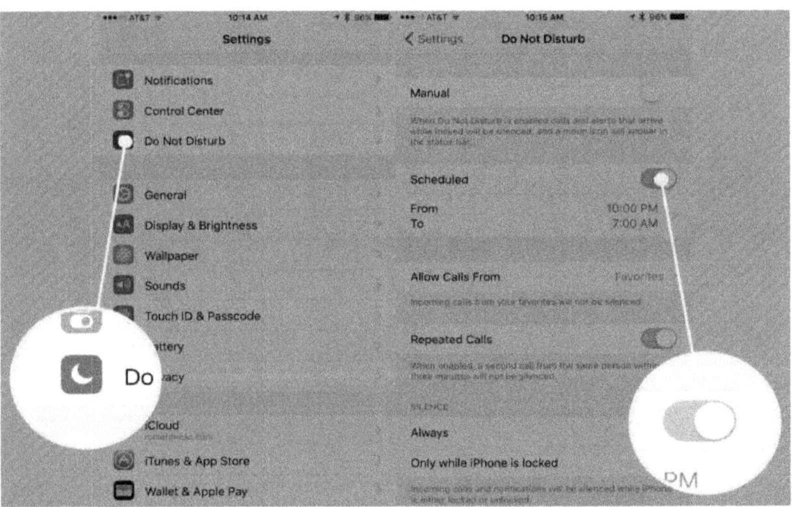

notifications.

From the Settings, switch the Scheduled to ON

In case of an emergency, let some apps on. For example, enable the **Allow Calls From your Favorites** and then toggle **Repeated Calls** to **ON**.

IV.   Customizing your iPhone with a retro ringtone

Having a distinctive ringtone allows the iPhone holders to be sure when their gadgets are ringing. It is advisable, therefore, to select an old-fashioned ringtone such as the xylophone. From the **Settings**, select the **Sound option**. Navigate downwards to the Classic (at the bottom of the list). Tap this **Classic icon** in order to provide a list of sounds from the original iPhones.

V.   Customization of the iPhone's name

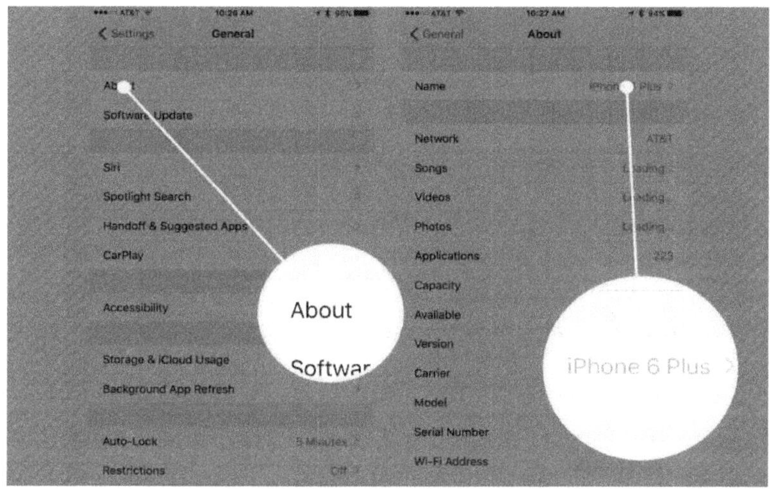

It is difficult to find your desired iPhone when using connected services such as the Find my iPhone. Changing the name of your brand-new iPhone is important for its easy identification. From the **Settings**, open the **General** icon and then **About**. Click on **Name** (this usually defaults to something imprecise). From this point, type in your desired brand name to make it easy to locate the handset while over the network.

Changing your iPhone's name

VI.   Using either the Touch ID or the Face ID to protect the content of the iPhone

The protection features that come with the Apple devices, including the Face ID in the iPhone X are important in ensuring that the content is safe from unauthorized personalities. Using such features include tapping into **Settings** then the **Touch ID option & Passcode** (Face ID and Passcode for the iPhone X). Make sure to turn **ON** the **iTunes & App Stores**, **Apple Pay,** and the **iPhone Unlock** before you can use the protection features that comes with the outstanding Apple products. Memorizing the password will not be necessary any longer once the Touch ID or Face ID feature is enabled.

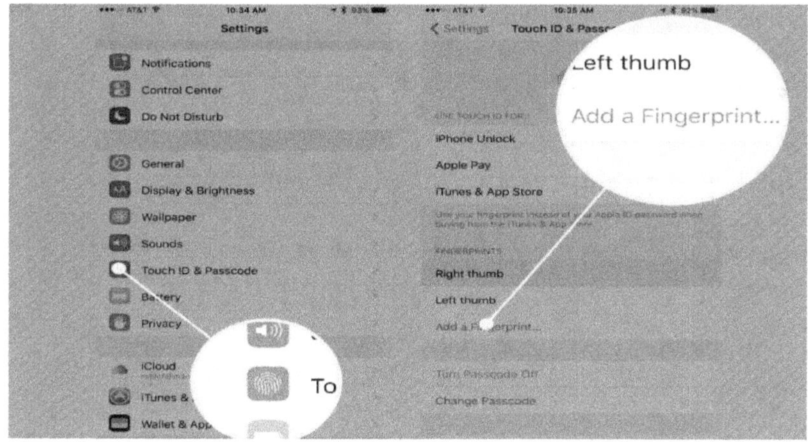

Make unlocking your phone easy by adding all your four fingers from each hand.

VII.   Email management

Managing email begins from adding the users' email accounts to set up their default accounts and to adding an HTML signature.

Adding of the email accounts - regardless of whether you are using the Google Inbox, Mail, Sparrow and the likes, it is mandatory to add your email accounts. For the Apple's Mail application, the adding procedure begins from the **Settings** then the **Accounts & Passwords**. This is followed by clicking of the **Add Account**. From here, the user is required to select his or her email provider.

Viewing of more preview - setting up a mail enables the users to see the contents of their messages without having to open them. From the **Settings**, click the **Mail** followed by tapping on the **Preview button**. For example, the user has the chance to change his or her settings to five lines in order to get more information from his or her emails

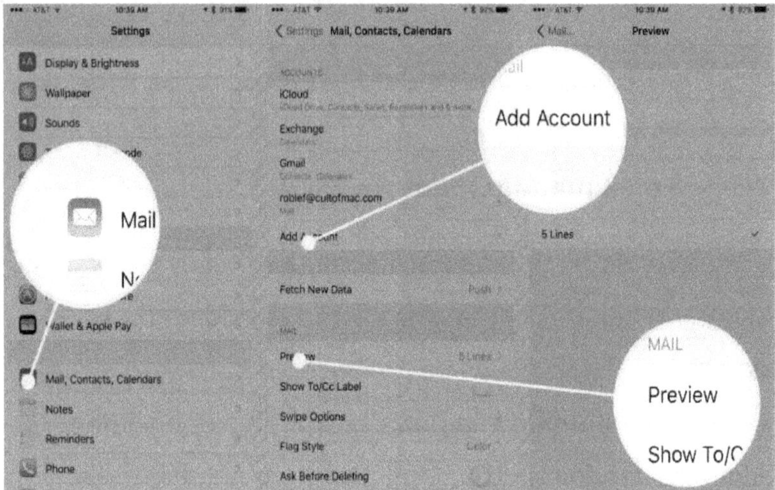

without having to open them.

Include your email accounts and be sure to see enough in the preview.

Set up your individual account - for some unexplainable factors, the iOS Mail settings sometimes defaults to an account like the iCloud, which we never use. The users need, therefore, to tap on the **Settings** then **Accounts & Passwords**. From this point, select **Your email account name**. Select the **Account** from the resulting display before concluding by clicking **Email**. Enter your personal email credentials that would be used as your *from an address* in the new mails.

Swiping away of unwanted mails - other than navigating through multiple buttons, the Swiping Option will help you manage your undesired mails. Change the **Swipe Right to Archive** to enable you save your mails to your archive. In case your email account has the **Swipe Left** as a default delete action, a **Trash** icon would be offered. Customization is advisable to change the **Swipe Left** to **Mark as Read** to avoid deleting important emails accidentally. This feature only works for the built-in Mail Apple app.

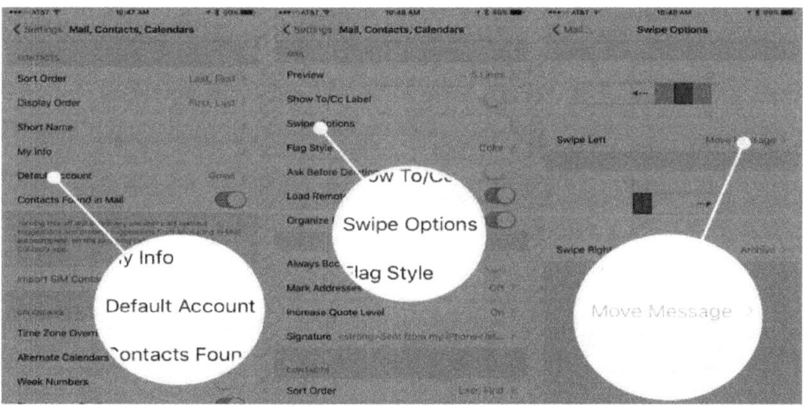

Set your preferred default email address as well as the swipe options.

Adding an HTML signature – adding this signature to the email brands the user's professionals. Depending on the users' preferences, the marks can either be simple text formatting tags or addition of a logo from a webserver. Although they would look clip-art-y and basic, an iOS app is useful when designing the signatures. In case you have one on your desktop, copy and paste the codes into an email and forward to yourself.

VIII.   Setting a default Calendar alert times

The calendar feature is vital in alerting the iPhone users of important events. It is recommendable to set default timing of special events like the birthdays, seminar dates and the other all-day events that would act as reminders to the users. To do this, therefore, navigate through the **Settings** app and locate the **Calendars**. From here, tap the **Default Alert Times** to set the reminders of different events.

Setting a birthday event one day before

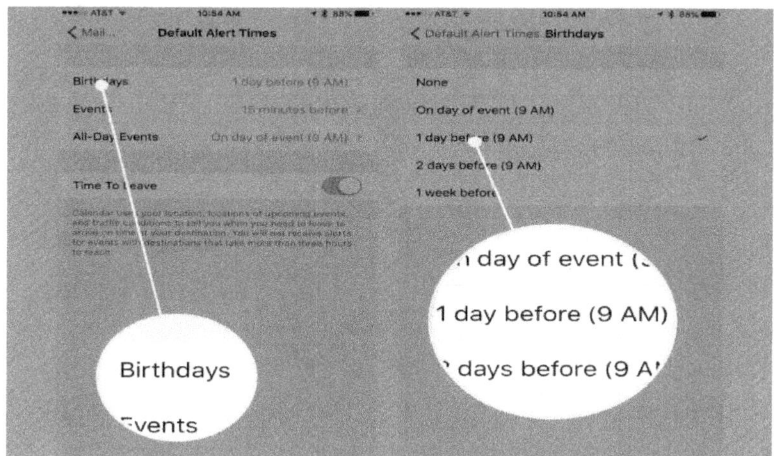

IX. Background app refresh

Selecting your preferred applications to display and run in the background. Open, therefore, the **Settings** app, select the **General**, and finally click on the **Background App Refresh** icon. From here, turn **ON** the Background App Refresh, while turning **OFF** all the other apps that you do not desire to run in the background.

X. Customizing your Control Center

Condensing the various utilities in a uniform-looking set of icons is a process enabled by the Control Center feature that comes with the iOS 11. Among the Apple's default Control Center features include the flashlight, alarm clock toggle for rotation screen lock, the Do Not Disturb, all the wireless controls (Airplane Mode, Wi-Fi and the Bluetooth), camera, calculator as well as the sliding controls of both the screen brightness and the device's volume.

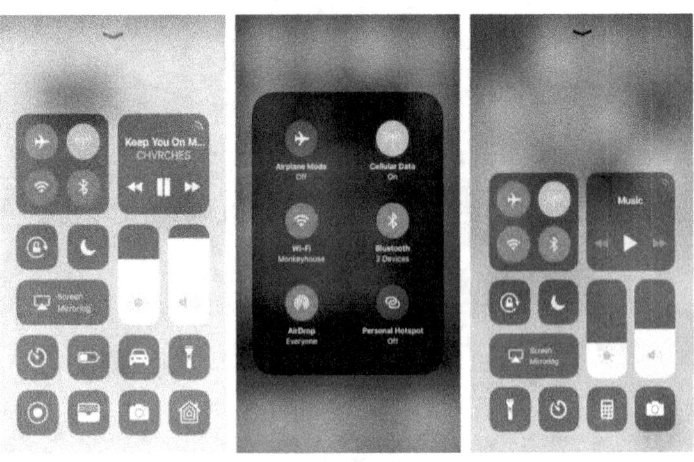

The iOS 11's Control Center is customizable, with the default configuration being at the far end.

All the Control Center utilities have hidden 3D Touch properties that expands upon long pressing on any of the controls. The prolonged pressing is considered because a simple tapping of the features would turn them on or off. According to its customizability, it is possible to add other features to the Control Center panel. From the **Settings** locate the **Control Center** and finally tap the **Customize Controls** icon that allows you to add any utility that interests you. Among the useful items to consider is the Screen Recording feature that records the content of the iPhone's screen to share with friends as well as the Do Not Disturb feature that will detect that you are in a moving vehicle.

XI.   Taking great photos

To take photos, simply open the camera app, focus on the object and then tap the on-screen shutter button for a shot. To keep with the competition with the rival companies, Apple includes some special features (lined along the left hand side of the app) that enhances the quality of the snap. These features can be turned either on or off depending on the preference of the gadget owner. The features include the following (from top to bottom):

Filters - this feature alters the color saturation among other factors to change the overall look of the photos upon shooting them.

Timer - this property allows you to take a group photo with the manager of the camera included. This benefit comes because of its ability to add either a 3-second or a 10-second timer.

Live Photo - this icon turns on and off the Apple's Live Photo mode.

HDR mode - this automatic feature helps in tricky contrast by simply taking of three photo shoots with different exposure levels and stitching them together to produce high-contrast photos with less murky areas and oversaturation.

Flash - photo shooting can continue after either turning the feature on, off or rather left in an auto mode.

It is also possible to quick-load the camera app without having to unlock the device. Simply tap the **iPhone's home or power button**, or alternatively raise the phone for the lock screen to display. **Swipe** your finger left across the device's screen to open the camera for shooting. In case, however, the gadget is already unlocked, flick your finger from the bottom of the screen to display the Control Center, with a camera icon located towards the bottom right corner.

XII.   Receiving text messages through your Mac or iPad

The outstanding iPhone releases include an iMessage feature. This property allows an iPhone to transfer its messages to an external platform like the Mac. To set up the feature on the other device, go to Settings and locate the Messages. From this point, turn on the iMessage on any iOS gadget. The already set device has to be close to the iPhone when setting your phone. This set up procedure is done by clicking the Settings and tap on Messages. The next procedure entails clicking on the Text Message Forwarding. From this stage, all the devices available will display. Turn on your Mac or the iPad, and check the target gadget to acquire its code that is finally entered into your personal iPhone to allowing all the messages to the other device: iPad or Mac.

CHAPTER FIVE: THE BENEFITS OF INVESTING IN THE LATEST IPHONE 8 AND X

Back in 2007 before the introduction of the first-ever iPhone, Nokia was the bestselling mobile device dealers globally. At $600, Apple introduced its first luxurious iPhone. Ten years down the line, the Apple devices influence our daily lives, institutions, boardrooms and the factories with more than 217 million handsets sold to date. As the most influential producers of consumer electronics products, the introduction of the iPhones 8, 8 Plus and the X by the Apple Company further transform the economic world.

Understanding the economic and social benefits of this technology innovation should be the driving factor for the acquisition of the iPhones 8 and X depending of what the Apple product lovers desire to achieve with the products. For that reason, this chapter highlights some of the special benefits of the iPhones in order to prove how worthy it is to invest on the products.

a) **A 24/7 internet connection for a successful business**

Strong internet connection is vital in order to carry on the majority of business activities, including the communication of important information. Unfortunately, internet outage decreases the productivity of the businesses, loss of customs among other negative effects.

Apple Company has joined the various providers of the internet is ushering in an age of all internet that provides a multitude of the communication platforms like the e-mail, Instagram, FaceTime, Facebook, Foursquare, Twitter as well as the Grindr. The connection provided in the iPhone is more reliable than the other mobile devices that have relatively limited internet access. The improved iPhone's browser similarly displays web pages as a desktop computer.

It is, therefore, economical for any business entrepreneur to consider acquiring an iPhone gadget to help him or her to enhance the productivity of his or her business operations regardless of an internet connection outage. The connection also help in the conduction of research of the various marketing strategies that would help in covering the expanded customer cloud for maximum profit.

   b) **The additional valuable apps that come with the latest iPhone 8 and iPhone X**

In addition to the tough and expansive glass touchscreen, iPhone introduces an iOS and a tightly controlled App Store (built-in Apple apps) that upon opening allow users to access the third-party apps that help them sync shopping lists, track the sun and act as a cash register among several other important uses.

The Apple Company having been given the mandate of controlling the app-approval and sales ecosystem to prevent the exposure of consumers to viruses and spam apps. For this reason, Apple ensures that all the excellent apps available are included in their products. It is, therefore, worthy to put your money on the company's product and be sure to enjoy the features that no other company handset brand can offer. For example, the App store has introduced a mini-economy app that is specialized for the business-oriented persons.

c) **iPhones introduces a new way of interacting with computers**

To replace the earlier physical keyboards and the numerical keypads, Apple introduced the iPhones that made the computing experience a simple dead procedure. That is, by the use of a few swipes of a finger, the iPhone holder can be able to navigate through his or her handset's contents. Just as in a computer, iPhones introduce a spell-checking feature, predictive-text software, cut (or copy) and paste as well as an innovative Siri voice-assistant features. This technology important for the recognizing voices has made it far much easier to speak questions and command instead of the usual tapping on the screen or keyboards.

As an alternative to buying a laptop or desktop computer, investing in iPhone is far much advisable because it supports diverse operations as the computer. One advantage is that it is portable and therefore does not inconvenience the owners. Conducting either the educational or the business-related researches is possible regardless of whether you are traveling or when in a seminar (confirming the reliability of some important facts).

d) iPhones gives you an option to store and protect your important contents.

The large internal space of the Apple product provides enough room to accommodate a large amount of data, including important documents, videos or even photos. The storage option allows the users to access their stored info at any time they would deem convenient.

The Touch ID (Face ID in iPhone X) and passcode options allows that only the authorized persons have the ability to access the contents. Paying more for a handset that would ensure maximum protection of your vital stuff.

e) The iPhones make the poor rich

Despite the high-cost tag that comes with the iPhones, the passionate enjoy an opportunity of multiplying their hard-earned cash following the purchase of the smartphones. For example, the use of the all-day internet connection allows the users to research on different business opportunities and ideas that could be beneficial for an improved well-being.

The information about the current market situation as well as strategies that the small-scale entrepreneurs could consider in expanding their businesses can also be accessed via the use of the default browser that comes with the iPhone. The device provides enough space for the business records.

f) The iPhones are quick and easy to use

Different smartphones come with unique features that require time to understand their uses. This means that users of these products have to be patient before enjoying their value. The Apple Company, fortunately, understands that time is a limited resource. Because of this, the layout of the device is simple, and with every feature having a clear symbol and name. This is unlike the Androids among the other devices available that come with confusing widgets and icons layout (the layout vary from one device to the next).

g) The smartphone has the ability to integrate with other Apple products

The inclusion of an Apple's iCloud integration property allows either the MacBook or the iPad holders to easily sync the phone content (documents, music or even photos) on the bigger screens. The users of the Windows laptops can also enjoy the benefit. The ability of the iPad handlers to switch on the automatic app download allows the applications already downloaded on the tablets to download automatically onto the iPhone as well.

Unlike the other smartphones such as the Android devices that lack this feature, the integration saves the users the expense they might have incurred for purchasing the internet connection for downloading the features. It is, therefore, cost-effective to consider purchasing an iPhone if you already own a MacBook or an iPad.

h) 24/7 customer service and technical support

Nothing disgusts more than purchasing an item that spoils even before you enjoy the value of its cost. It further pains when you do not have the contact of the support team in case of any technical or any other assistance about the smartphone. iPhone beats all the other existing gadgets because of the availability of a competent support team that is ever ready to provide assistance in case of any issue with your device.

In case of any issue such as the difficulty in setting up your personal email, simply book an appointment at any local Apple Store and the staff would provide you with the free technical advice regarding the issue. Your phone is replaced with another one in case it has been found to be faulty during the transaction. For this reason, it is important to invest where you feel your money is safe. That is, consider the excellent Apple handset to be sure that your value is upheld.

With the additional outstanding features, the extra cost covers for the features that when utilized effectively will ensure that your sweat was never in vain. It is, therefore, worthy investing your hard-earned resources on the iPhone devices for a residual and successful business endeavor.

CHAPTER SIX: THE COMMON TROUBLESHOOTING SOLUTIONS FOR THE IPHONE 8 AND X

The introduction of the iPhones 8 and X targets to improve the global economy through providing a good communication network and research platform. The features of the Apple products are so outstanding and aesthetically acceptable to the customers. Despite the items being the best in the market, the curious users have reported some of the issues that might repel most users (both software and hardware).

For this reason, this chapter highlights some of the common issues and their troubleshooting solutions for a more reliable experience with the product.

a. Failure of the software to update

Every time the iOS is updating, serial errors occur. That is, "Software Update Failed. An error occurred downloading iOS 11" or "Software Update Failed. An error occurred installing iOS 11". The issue is universal and hence the need to fix it early enough.

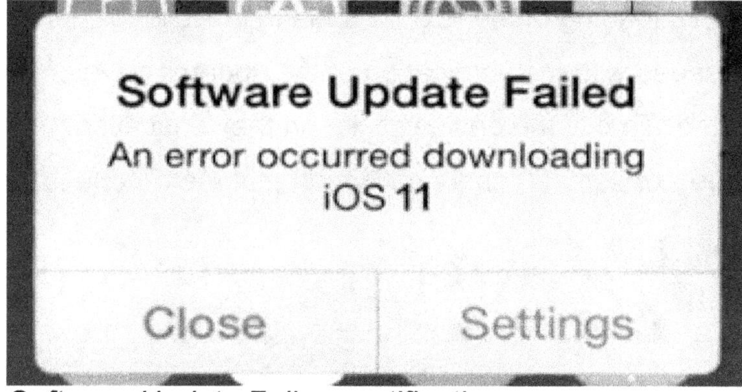

Software Update Failure notification

Solution

- ➢ To fix the problem, you have first to confirm that your iPhone supports the iOS 11.
- ➢ Being sure that your device is compatible, the next procedure entails conducting a Reset Network Settings. To do this, visit the **Settings** then select **General**, then **Reset** before finally tapping on the **Reset Network Settings** option.
- ➢ One done, force a Restart on Your Device by pressing and holding both the Home and power buttons until the Apple logo appears.
- ➢ Turn off the Wi-Fi and switch to the cellular data before using the iTunes to update the iOS 11 on your computer.

b. Verification of the update issues

Once the downloading of the iOS 11 updating files is complete, issues with the verification of the updates have been reported. That is the device sticks on the verification update screen or sometimes a notification that the iPhone is

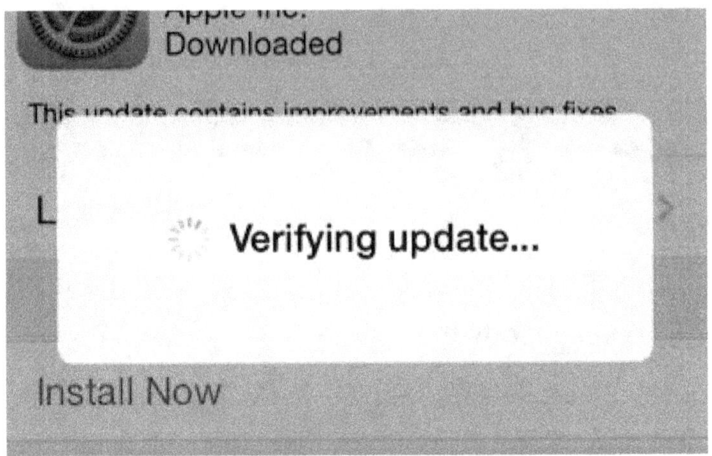

not able to verify the update.

The device is sticking on the verifying update screen.

Solution

With the device connected to an active connection, either hard reset or reboot your gadget.

Once the reset is successful, update the iOS 11 via the iTunes on your computers.

c. **Unavailability of enough space to download updates**

Insufficient Space For Download

In order to make room for the
software update, some apps will need
to be temporarily deleted. All deleted
apps will automatically be replaced
after the update is complete. Would
you like to continue?

Cancel

Allow App Deletion

As the iOS 8 requires up to 5 GB, only the devices with either

16GB or the 32GB storage space support the iOS 11.

Notification about the insufficient space for the update

Solutions

The most common solution entails transferring data from the

iPhone to another iOS gadget.

Backing up of the data with iTunes creates space for the

updates. Since the large files cost much time, however, the

iTunes alternative- AnyTrans selectively transfer data and

create room for the downloading of the updates.

   d. **Fast draining battery**

Every time an upgrade is done on the iOS, the consumers complain of the devices consuming a large amount of power at an extremely faster rate.

Notification of critically low battery status

Solution

The first step entails restarting your device. This is done by turning off the power button before powering it on again. Consider using the Low Power Mode to minimize the power usage by the phone. To do this, navigate the **Settings** app and locate the **Battery** then locate and turn on the **Low Power Mode**.

- ❖ Disabling the widgets is another strategy to minimize the consumption of energy while using your device. To manage them, swipe to the right while on the home screen. From here scroll to the bottom of the widgets and select **Edit**. From here, deactivate the widget by

clicking on a red circle that appears with white lines. Confirm the operation by tapping **Remove**.

❖ Resetting all the setting is another way to control the consumption of energy. To do this, visit the **Settings** > **General** > **Reset** > **Reset All Settings** and then enter your passcode before confirming the process.

❖ To turn off the background app refresh (consumes extra power) go to **General** from the **Settings** app before selecting the **Background App Refresh** and then turn it off.

❖ Disabling the Raise to Wake is also a way of minimizing the energy consumption. To do this, visit the **Settings** app then locate the **Display & Brightness** before turning off the **Raise to Wake** option.

e. Charging issues

After upgrading to iOS 11, many users complain of their devices not recognizing USB for charging or rather charge slowly.

Solution

A number of solutions that prove to be useful when it comes to rectifying the issue:

- Hard reset your iPhone.
- Consider using an Apple-matched USB cable.
- Confirm that the USB cable is in a good state.
- Using an iPad charger charges the iPhones faster.

f. The overheating of the iPhone

Most users of the iPhones complain of the temperature too high warning, and it is advisable to cool the gadget during updating before using them.

Extreme temperature warning

Solutions

- Wait for the phone to cool down automatically, turn it off, reset it, or download the update once again.
- Turn off the GPS (heats up the iPhone) by navigating to **Settings** and then **Privacy** followed by **Location Service** before tapping the **Off** option.
- Another obvious strategy is to take off the case of the iPhone to help cool it.

g. Cellular data issues

Another issue that has been experienced in iPhones is the cellular data being strangely slow, or sometimes not working with the iOS 11.

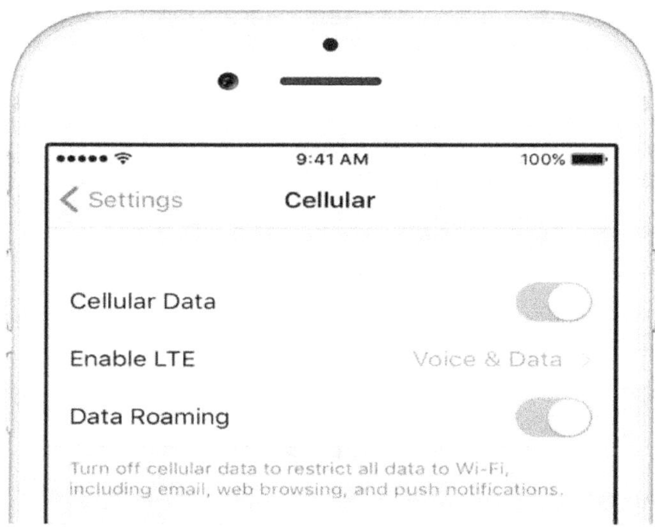

Cellular data issue

Solutions

- Confirm first with your carrier to determine in case of an outage within the area. To do this, go to **Settings** then select the **About** display the details.
- Restart your device. To do this, turn off the power button then on again.
- Turn off the cellular data for a few seconds before turning it on again.
- Enable the Airplane mode for about 30 seconds before turning it off. To do this, visit the **Control Center** then click on the **Turn On Airplane Mode** option.

- o Reset Network Settings. The rest is done from the **Settings** then locate the **General** then **Reset** and finally the **Reset Network Settings**.

h. Sound issues

I have heard complains about the sound suddenly cuts out when the users are using the outstanding applications.

Solutions

- ➢ Restart the iPhone by turning it off then on the after a few seconds.
- ➢ Turn the Bluetooth on and off to see whether it would rectify the issue.
- ➢ Confirm that the debris of the speaker grille is not the cause of the issue. In case of any foreign matter, remove it to improve the device's sound.
- ➢ If a specific app has the sound problem, download the latest version and rectify the issue.

i. Issues with downloading and updating the apps

Sometimes, the apps face troubles when downloading and updating.

Issue downloading an app

Unable to Download App

"AirShou" could not be installed at this time.

| Done | Retry |

Solutions

> Restart the iPhone and then try to download the app again

> In case of a persistent problem, click the **Update** on the app before the **Open** symbol appears.

j. Losing of data after carrying out an update

Upon every upgrading of the iOS, some users complain of the losing their photos, music among their other important documents.

Recovering the lost data

Solutions

To help the users keep their important data, it is advisable to back up their iPhones with the iTunes or other iTunes-alternatives like the AnyTrans before beginning the upgrade processes. This step allows them to recover their lost data in case they are lost after the operation.

In case your content is not backed up, fortunately, use a PhoneRescue software to recover the lost data.

k. Finding it difficult to turn on your iPhone

Upon upgrading your Apple device, sometimes affects the phone in that it does not turn on.

Phone not turning on

Solutions

> ➢ Connect the iPhones to the power source for some time before trying to turn it on
> ➢ Consider performing a hard reset
> ➢ Force the device into a Recovery Mode

- ➢ Alternatively, you can put the iPhone into the DFU Mode
- ➢ Restore the iPhone with iTunes

I. **The notifications appearing incorrectly**

Upgrading of the iPhones to iOS 11 might cause them to display notifications in undesirable format. That is, the display appears to be chopped up and separated from the top, middle and bottom of the screen.

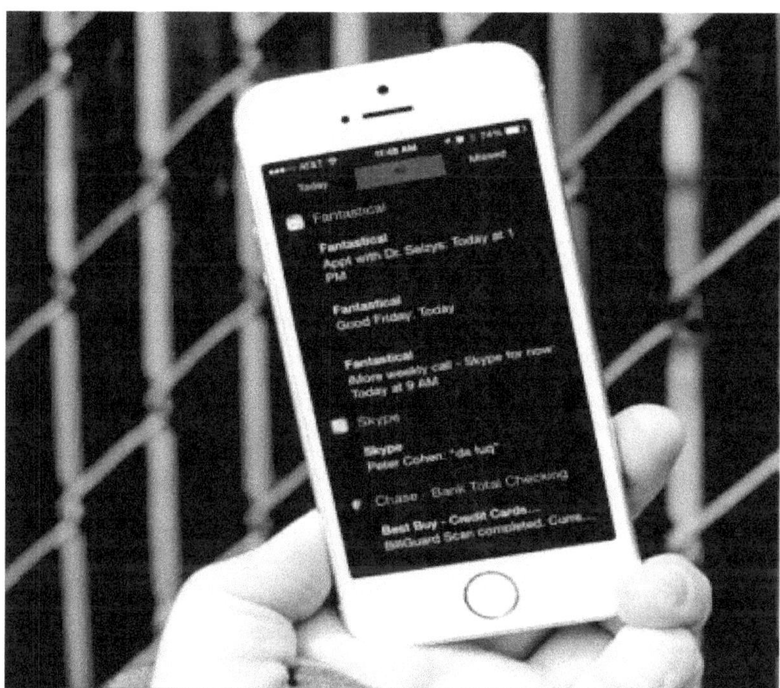

Incorrectly displayed notifications

Solutions

Simultaneously press and hold the Home and the Sleep/Wake buttons for about ten seconds until the Apple logo displays.

Alternatively, force press the "x" that displays on the notification screen to clear all the on-screen notifications. Wait for a new notification to confirm whether the problem persists.

m. The inability of the iPhone to either call or receive calls

For some technical reasons, the users of the iPhones experience the problem of making calls or receiving calls.

Solution

In case you experience the problems, the following strategies can help in the management of issues:

- ➢ Reset the Network Settings
- ➢ Remove and re-insert the Sim card
- ➢ Update your carrier
- ➢ Try restoring your iPhone
- ➢ Verify the blocked phone numbers

Many problems (not limited to the highlighted ones) hinder the enjoyment of the outstanding features that are included in the iPhones. For that reason, it is not possible to highlight all the issues and their remedies. Considering the following procedures' therefore, helps in fixing most of the iOS problems:

1. Upon experiencing an issue with your iPhone for the first time, restart or reset the gadget by simultaneously long-pressing both the Sleep/Wake and the Home buttons until the Apple logo displays.

2. For network issues, go to the Settings and then Reset. From here, select the Reset Network Settings to default the network settings.
3. In case the problems persist, open the Settings App and locate General then Reset. From here, select Reset All Settings to restore the phone to the default settings.
4. If any of the three options do not work, restore your iPhone by plugging it into a computer that runs iTunes. The restoration will delete the calendars, contacts, and photos among several other data on the handset. However, the backed-up data will automatically information such as the text messages and the contact favorites.

CONCLUSION

Ever since the introduction into the market in 2007, Apple Company has endeavored to upgrade its products in order to meet the global customers' desires. That is the introduction of new and outstanding features enhanced at ensuring that the users have a memorable experience with the handsets. The product upgrading as well maintains a healthy competition with the rival companies such as the Samsung and LG Companies. The latest addition to the iPhones the 8, the 8 Plus and the X, for example, comes with features like the Face ID to safeguard the content of your gadget.

The many features are only important if the users have a vast knowledge about them. For that reason, this book has highlighted some of the special features that define the releases. The differences between the iPhone 8 and the iPhone X are as well made clear in the book to allow the Apple product lovers to select the one they deem to match their individual desires or meet their economic capabilities. Detailed information about how to get the best out of the features is vital in boosting the productivity of your business and any other function that you need the phone. For example, appropriate usage of the default browser of the iPhones can help students conduct research on different research topics. Business people also use the feature to get a clue on how to compete the global competitors.

Despite the significant importance of the latest handsets, the long-term users of the iPhones have identified some of the common issues that hinder the productivity of the products. A chapter of this book, therefore, has chosen some of the common issues that have been reported for a long time by most users of the phone model and the various steps that would help in rectifying your gadget for a valuable purchase. Another special chapter of this publication also explains the reason why it is worthy to invest on the iPhone. It is, therefore, important to consider going through the contents of this book to help you in seeing the value of the money you have worked hard to make.